DATE DUE

APR 19 1995

MAY 17 1995

GAYLORD

PRINTED IN U.S.A.

Kizer, Katheryn W.
THe Harley Shields: Alaskan
Missionaries

The
Harley Shields:
Alaskan Missionaries

KATHRYN W. KIZER

Illustrated by Jack Woodson

BROADMAN PRESS
Nashville, Tennessee

Thanks

To Harley and Martha Shield. They
showed me what it is like to be
missionaries.
To Chuck and Russell, my sons. They
helped me learn about children.
To Lawton, my husband. He is my
partner in ministry.

© Copyright 1984 • Broadman Press
All rights reserved
4242-85
ISBN: 0-8054-4285-5
Dewey Decimal Classification: J266.092
Subject Headings: SHIELD, HARLEY / / SHIELD, MARTHA / / MISSIONS—ALASKA
Library of Congress Catalog Card Number: 84-5821
Printed in the United States of America

Library of Congress Cataloging in Publication Data

Kizer, Kathryn W., 1924-
   The Harley Shields.

   Summary: A biography of Alaskan missionaries, Harley
and Martha Shields, with emphasis on how they became
missionaries and on their work with the Eskimos.
   1. Shields, Harley—Juvenile literature.   2. Shields,
Martha Ellenwood—Juvenile literature.   3. Missionaries—Alaska—Biography—Juvenile literature.
4. Missions—Alaska—Juvenile literature.   5. Eskimos—
Alaska—Missions—Juvenile literature.   [1. Shields,
Harley.   2. Shields, Martha Ellenwood.   3. Missionaries.   4. Eskimos—Alaska—Missions]   I. Woodson,
Jack, ill.   II. Title.
BV2765.5.A1K59   1984   266'.61'0922 [B] [920]   84-5821
ISBN 0-8054-4285-5

Contents

Harley Grows Up

"Get back, Bobby," said Harley. He cupped
his hands around his mouth to whisper.
"Someone will see you."

Harley sat in the dark corner of his garage.
Bobby, his friend, cracked the door to peep out.
All morning the boys had been quiet—hiding in
the garage.

"No one has found us yet," said Bobby.

"Wonder what they are doing at school today?"
asked Harley. "Skipping school isn't as much fun
as I thought it would be."

The boys drew pictures on the dirt floor with
their fingers. That helped pass the time.

Squeak! The garage door flew open. There
stood Mrs. Shield, Harley's mother.

"What are you boys doing in here? Why aren't
you in school?" Her words came very fast. And
her face was red. The boys knew she was mad.

"Mom, you know I always get caught," were
Harley's first words. "Every time I do anything
wrong, I get caught."

Harley was born on Mother's Day, May 13, 1923. He grew up in Santa Barbara, California. He had two brothers. One was older, and one was younger. Harley was in the middle. He was tall and thin. He had thick, black hair that never looked combed.

All through the school years, Harley never liked to study. He was happy when he reached the last year of high school. One day near graduation, the principal stopped him in the hall. "You have changed this year, Harley," Mr. Holt said. "You showed your teachers you could make better grades. I'm proud of you."

Martha as a Girl

"This is fun," said Martha to Esther, her sister. Each girl walked on two tin cans. Their hands held the ropes to lift the cans.

"Help me, Martha. I'm about to fall," laughed Esther. The ropes around Esther's cans were loose.

Martha quickly let go of her ropes. She ran to Esther. "Pull the ropes tight," she told her. "You can do it."

Martha and Esther were buddies. They liked to do things together.

Every member of the Ellenwood family liked to read. Many Sunday afternoons Martha's mom and dad took their three girls to the library.

"I love Betty Gordon mysteries," said Martha. "I can't wait to read this one."

"Will you tell me about it?" asked Shirley, Martha's much-younger sister.

"I know she will," said Mr. Ellenwood. "But come here a minute, girls. Let me show you these pictures in my book. This is where we went camping last summer."

Camping was fun for the Ellenwood family. Martha liked the out of doors.

Martha liked to play baseball. "We want Martha on our team," girls often said. "She's a good hitter." She was also one of the tallest girls in her class.

Methodist Church Party

After high school, Harley worked for the Western Pacific Railroad. When he was nineteen, he went with a friend to Anchorage, Alaska. He wrote to his mom: "I really like Alaska. I have decided to stay here. Good news! I have a job with the Alaska Railroad making a dollar an hour."

At twenty-one, Harley went into the United States Army. For two years, he lived in many different places. It was a happy day in 1946 when he got out of the Army.

"Now I must look for a job," he told his family. It was not easy to find a job in Santa Barbara, California. Finally, he went to work for a gas company. His job was digging ditches.

One day Dick, Harley's younger brother, said, "Harley, you stay home too much. Will you go with me to the Methodist church Tuesday night? They are having a big party."

"I'll think about it and let you know," he told Dick. Harley was bashful. He didn't like to talk to strangers.

But Tuesday night Harley was ready to go. Off the two brothers went in Harley's car. It was a 1936 blue sports car with a rumble seat. Dick wanted Harley to meet his new friend Martha.

It was an exciting evening. There were games and music—talking and laughing. Harley didn't want the party to end.

"Let me take you home," he said to Martha. "We'll go by Dopey's for ice cream."

"OK, but Sister must come too," Martha replied.

Harley's mother and a friend came into the restaurant.

"Isn't that Harley at that table?" asked Mrs. Shield's friend. "There are two girls with him."

"We didn't know he knew any girls. I can't believe he is with two," said Mrs. Shield.

Harley saw Martha every week. He liked to talk with her on the telephone. He liked to walk in the moonlight with her. Seven months went by.

One night Harley felt very brave. He knew he loved Martha. He thought she loved him.

"Will you marry me?" he asked her. He had a ring to slip on her finger.

Martha loved Harley. She said she would marry him. He put the ring on her finger.

On a hot August afternoon in 1947, Martha and Harley were married. It was a double wedding at the Methodist church where they had met. Esther, Martha's sister, and her boyfriend were married too.

What good memories for Martha and Harley!
There were baskets of flowers and white candles.
The two sisters wore matching satin dresses.
After the wedding, Harley and Martha left in his
blue car.

On an Indian Reservation

Harley wanted to go to college. The government would pay for this because he had been in the Army.

"If I work part time, we'll have enough money," Harley told Martha. "I will get $108 a month from the government."

"I think we can make it," said Martha. "We don't pay much rent. Surely that will buy food for us."

So Harley started to college in Idaho. Later they moved back to California. He went to school there. Four busy, hard years went by.

"Whoopee!" Harley said as he held his diploma in his hand. "Look out, world. I'm ready for work."

Harley took a job teaching school on Hoopa [HOOP-ah] Indian Reservation. He and Martha rented a one-room shack with no inside bath. By now Harley and Martha had three children. They were Bonnie, Ted, and Lou Ann.

One day Miss Juanita Frey, an Indian, invited the Shields to the Presbyterian Indian Mission. It was the week of revival. A visiting preacher spoke every night.

On Wednesday night, Martha went to the front of the little church. "I want Jesus as my Savior," she told the preacher.

The next night at the end of the sermon, the preacher asked, "Does anyone here want to follow Jesus?"

At once, Harley spoke up. "I do," he said. Everyone looked at Harley and smiled. He did not know not to speak aloud in church. He wanted the people to know he needed God in his life.

14

Joining the Baptist Church

Harley taught school for several years on the Hoopa Reservation. Martha took care of their children.

Then the family moved to Portland, Oregon. Harley wanted to go to Multnomah School of the Bible in Portland. That summer they had no house and lived in a tent. Their son Larry was born in July.

For a long time, Harley had felt God wanted him to do some special work. He did not know what it was. He and Martha prayed a lot.

When fall came, the Shield family moved into a house. On Sundays they went to a little Baptist church near their home. Joe Smith, the preacher, talked about tithing. He talked about how Jesus asks us to tell others about him. Harley agreed with what he heard.

"We want to join the Baptist church," Harley and Martha told Mr. Smith.

Life was hard in Portland. Often there was not enough food to eat. The children needed shoes and clothes. Larry became sick.

"Lord, we need some help," the parents prayed.

A man from the church came to see them just before Christmas. "I'm not going to ask how you're getting along," the man said. "I want to see inside your cupboard. I want to know if you have enough to eat."

It was a happy day when the man came back to their home. He brought food, clothes, and toys.

Bonnie looked at her mother. She saw tears in her mom's eyes. Bonnie knew her mother had asked God to make this a happy Christmas.

"You got just what you asked for, Mother," Bonnie said happily.

Back to Hoopa

Harley finished school at the Bible college. Then the family moved back to Hoopa, the Indian reservation. Harley taught school. He never made much money. He drove the school bus to make extra money.

Harley and Martha started several churches on the reservation. Sometimes a church met in their home. Sometimes their home was in the church building. They had Vacation Bible School under a walnut tree. Harley preached every Sunday in many different places.

"I cannot go on like this. Teaching school and preaching are too much," Harley said.

"What do you suggest we do?" Martha asked.

"I have made up my mind. I will go to Golden Gate Seminary," he said. "I want to study to become a better preacher."

To the Seminary

Harley was on the way to the seminary office. He felt in his pocket. He had only five dollars and a gasoline credit card.

The man in the seminary office said, "You need eighty dollars. Are you ready to pay?"

"No," said Harley. "I don't have that much money."

"Well, it looks like you will have to save some. Then come back."

Harley walked to his car. He was sad as he backed out of the parking lot. Then he saw Rafael, a Cuban friend. Harley had met Rafael at a summer Bible camp. He was now a student in the seminary.

"Are you coming to school here?" Rafael asked.

Harley told him he needed eighty dollars. Rafael said, "Come back to the office with me. I will help you get in."

And he did! Harley lived in the men's dormitory at first. He ate peanut butter and crackers almost every day. He got a part-time job at a gas station.

This time was hard for Martha. She and Harley had six children now. Martha and the children lived with her sister for a while. Later Harley and Martha rented a small house. Martha got a job working at night.

Harley drove thirty miles to the seminary each day. One day he said, "Martha, I'm sorry you have to go to work as soon as I get home. You are too good to me." He put his arms around her. "Thank you for helping me go to the seminary."

Harley graduated from the seminary in 1962. The Home Mission Board asked Harley and Martha to be home missionaries. They went to work with the Indians at the Hoopa Reservation.

A Trip to Alaska

In 1965 Harley began to think about his days in Alaska. That was a long time ago. But he still remembered. One day he wrote William Hanson, the director of Alaskan Baptists. Later, Mr. Hanson called Harley. "How would you like to move to Kotzebue? We need a pastor there."

Harley and Martha looked at the map. They found that Kotzebue is way up in the Arctic area. That is the coldest part of Alaska.

Finally they told Mr. Hanson they would go. But the Home Mission Board did not approve the move. It was the Board who would pay his salary.

"You have too many children. Life is rough there. It is too cold," the people at the Board told Harley. "The last missionary we sent would not stay."

The next spring, Harley decided to go to Alaska on his own. He would look for a job. He could pay his own way as a missionary. He had $190 when he drove to Seattle, Washington. From there he took a plane to Fairbanks, Alaska. He got a motel room in Fairbanks. When he counted his money the next day, he had sixty cents.

There was a knock at the motel door. "Hello, Harley. I've been looking for you," said J. T. Burdine. He was the pastor of the University Baptist Church in Fairbanks. "Brother Hanson sent me some money. He wants me to buy groceries for you."

For two months, Harley stayed at the Fort Yukon Mission in Alaska. Every day he looked for work. But he had no luck. Finally, he went back to Hoopa.

Five months went by. Harley and Martha were

sad. He said to his wife, "I will write the Home Mission Board one more time. I want to know if they have a pastor at Kotzebue."

Harley wrote a five-page letter. He told the people at the Home Mission Board ways his children could take care of themselves. He told the Board that God wanted him to work in Alaska.

Three weeks later Harley and Martha got a letter. It said, "People at the Home Mission Board have talked again. We have agreed to send you to Alaska."

The Shields in Kotzebue

On June 18, 1966, the Shield family stepped off the airplane. They were in Kotzebue, Alaska. Their home was to be in the church building.

Nothing in the house worked right. The furnace did not work. The oil stove for cooking was out of order. Harley spent the next two weeks fixing things. There was no one in Kotzebue to do the work.

On Sunday, the Shields were ready for Sunday School. Martha had about ten Eskimo children in her class. They were very noisy. Every time

she tried to speak, they talked too.

In the middle of the class, Martha stopped. "Why did you boys and girls come to Sunday School?" she asked. "I cannot teach until you are ready to learn."

She ran to her kitchen. Tears ran down her cheeks.

After a few minutes, she returned to the children. Everyone was quiet when she entered the room. The boys and girls knew she wanted to help them.

Harley was pastor of the Kotzebue First Baptist Church for ten years. The Shields had camps for children. Martha had slumber parties for the girls. Harley went ice-skating and did other things with the boys. They took groups snow-machining.

The Shield children learned to wear a lot of heavy clothes and boots in Kotzebue. Sometimes it was so cold that they couldn't move their fingers and toes. They learned to eat moose and caribou meat.

In 1973 Jack Maxwell of Texas said to Harley, "What you need is an airplane. It takes too long and it's too cold to travel by dogsled and snowmobile. Come visit me in Texas. I will teach you to fly."

Harley was excited. "I could really get out to the Eskimo villages if I had a plane," he said.

"We will ask God," said Martha. "He always gives us what we need."

And God did! They found a good buy on a two-passenger plane. Some Christians from the other states gave some money. Some churches in Alaska gave money too. Harley got a loan at the bank for the rest of the money to buy the plane.

Traveling to Eskimo Villages

The Kotzebue church started missions in many Eskimo villages. Harley traveled to these missions. He took his guitar to help the people sing. He preached. He visited people in their cabins.

"Martha, I feel we need to move to one of these villages," Harley said. "Maybe the Home Mission Board would send another missionary to Kotzebue."

"You're right," said Martha. "I don't think the Board will find anyone who will go to the villages. But you already love these Eskimos, Harley. I will do what you and God think best."

In 1976 the Shields moved to Selawik. This is a small village. It is seventy miles east of Kotzebue. They lived in three rooms behind the church. They had no running water. They had no television. They listened to news on the radio. They had no telephone. They talked to others by CB radio.

Harley and Martha travel a lot in their work. They go to the other villages by plane or snowmobile. When ready for a plane trip, Harley calls on the CB: "Selawik 2. This is 0651. How is the wind in Kiana?"

Then he puts his long hunting knife in his belt. He always packs a tent. He puts in sleeping bags and animal skins. Harley and Martha go prepared for whatever might happen. They wear parkas (heavy coats) and mukluks (lined boots).

Usually they stay a couple of days in each village. They sleep in the little village churches. They have Bible studies and worship services. Sometimes only five or six Eskimos come. At times, Martha and Harley get discouraged.

"We must never give up," Harley said once. "Our work is just the beginning. Only God knows the ending. We must count on him to work in the lives of these people."

At another time Harley was talking to the people. It was a time that was very sad for their family. Harley said: "We came to Alaska as missionaries years ago. Our children grew up here. They have married your children. One of our children has died here. This is our home. We will stay here and work for God."

ARCTIC OCEAN

ARCTIC CIRCLE

○ KIANA
○ KOTZEBUE
○ SELAWIK

FAIRBANKS
●

ALASKA

ANCHORAGE
●

PACIFIC OCEAN

Remember

God helped Harley and Martha Shield get ready to work for him in Alaska. Remember the hard times they had on the Hoopa Indian Reservation. How did this help them with the hard times in Alaska?

Harley and Martha were already married before they knew Jesus. Who invited them to church? That was important for them. Do you know someone you can invite to your church?

Remember to pray for missionaries. Pray for the Shields. Pray for yourself. Ask God to help you become all that he wants you to be.

About the Author

Kathryn Kizer is an editor with Woman's Missionary Union in Birmingham, Alabama. She has also been Preschool and Children's director for several churches.

Her husband, Lawton, is a minister of education. They have been on many mission trips together. They went to Alaska in August, 1982. The best part of that trip was spending two days with Harley and Martha Shield. They are special.